There's MAGIC in the AIR

A PILOT'S BEHIND-THE-SCENES VIEW OF AVIATION

by David Visser

- a storybook for kids
- a textbook for adults
- an explanation of aviation for the young and old

Clovercroft Publishing

There's Magic in the Air: A Pilot's Behind-the-Scenes View of Aviation

Published by Clovercroft Publishing, Franklin, Tennessee

Illustrated by Brandon Bolt

Cover Design by Suzanne Lawing

Interior Design by Adept Content Solutions

Edited by Tammy Kling

Printed in the United States of America

978-1-942557-12-8

Contents

Introduction

Flying seems magical.

Even after all these years as a pilot I'm still enthusiastic about working inside the cockpit, soaring through the clouds. When you fly you have a feeling of being suspended above the earth, gliding through blue skies.

But aviation is perhaps one of the few industries that's magical for everyone, even those who don't work in it. Is it the shiny planes? Is it the beauty and majesty of the skies? Is it the feeling of flight, or the momentum of the journey itself? I think it's a combination of all of those things.

I didn't always want to be a pilot. The first three and a half years of my life, I didn't know what I wanted to do. At six months old, I was busy moving from Massachusetts to Vermont. I decided to leave the driving up to my father. At one, I was busy cutting teeth, eating regular food and working on that drooling thing. One and a half to two years old was that whole walking thing. In my twos I decided to act out a little. It wasn't until I was about three and a half that I started pointing to the sky and found my passion for aviation. I announced I was going to be a pilot. It was quite confusing when everyone patted me on the head, smiled and said, "That's nice." Let's go folks! I wanna get my pilots license. Unbeknownst to me, I'd have to wait another 14 years before realizing my dream.

Pistol Pete Maravich says in the movie "The Pistol, The Birth of a Legend", that all you need to succeed is Desire, Discipline and Dedication (www.the pistolmovie.com). Even though I wouldn't fly an aircraft by myself for another 14 years, I kept my Desire to fly alive. My journey was about to begin. The Discipline and Dedication would come later…

When you step onto an airplane you're on a journey, traveling to a special destination, or taking a vacation somewhere new. This process of going from point A to point B can seem filled with mystery to the average person, with all of the complexity involved in the process of flying: the aircraft, airport security, communication with the tower, and the way the ground personnel communicate with the pilots and aviation professionals in the air.

Throughout this book I hope to demystify some of the magic of flying, and educate you about the intricacies of aviation. From planes, to lift, to turbulence, to the process of flight, you'll learn many different facets of the industry that you weren't aware of before!

But before you begin…

Take a look at the back cover.

The aircraft I fly is called a Piaggio Avanti II. Thousands of hours of wind tunnel testing were used in order to create this design. Each curve or smooth line has a reason behind it. For example, the aircraft has a forward wing which creates approximately 18% of the total lift, which is what is used to keep the nose in the air.

The body or fuselage itself creates approximately 20% of the lift. This allows the engineers to decrease the main wing by over a third of its size. In level flight, the tail creates practically no lift at all. With these factors combined, induced drag was decreased greatly. Induced drag is a by-product of lift. This allows this type of aircraft to fly faster and more efficiently. Now that might sound like a lot of aviation lingo to you but basically that means that engineers have thought long and hard about how to design a specific aircraft! Engineers and scientists are constantly looking for ways to improve aircraft design.

As you'll learn in these pages, there's a lot that happens even before a passenger steps onto the plane. Buckle your seatbelt, and come along for the ride. I'm going to show you what's behind the scenes in aviation!

Hey kids! Meet Johnny and Jamie Jet! They're going to help us learn about the magical world of aviation. You'll find them on the left-hand page of the book. The right hand page is for the grown-ups to read and explain more of what is happening in the picture.

Interspersed throughout the book you will find a series of quotes. The first four deal with authors and the writing of aviation. The rest show the progression of aviation over time, starting with the first untethered hot air balloon flight in 1783. These quotes can be read in sequence by skipping to the page number listed at the bottom.

"The shape of my wing lets me fly!"

How Airplanes Fly

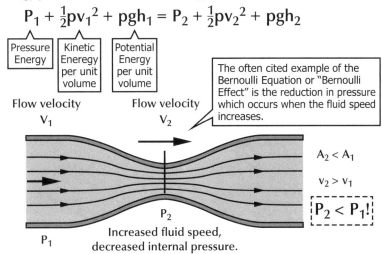

Energy per unit volume before = Energy per unit volume after

$$P_1 + \tfrac{1}{2}pv_1{}^2 + pgh_1 = P_2 + \tfrac{1}{2}pv_2{}^2 + pgh_2$$

Pressure Energy

Kinetic Eneregy per unit volume

Potential Energy per unit volume

The often cited example of the Bernoulli Equation or "Bernoulli Effect" is the reduction in pressure which occurs when the fluid speed increases.

Flow velocity V_1

Flow velocity V_2

$A_2 < A_1$

$v_2 > v_1$

$P_2 < P_1!$

P_2

P_1

Increased fluid speed, decreased internal pressure.

The Bernoulli equation

What a great way to start a book!

Let's talk about lift.

On every page you will find a physics equation for you to study. Each one more difficult. There will be a test at the end. No no, I'm just kidding! Pilot humor. Although pilots actually do have to understand this equation, you don't! So let's see if I can explain lift a little easier here than the above equation.

"You've just created lift!"

The airflow around a plane's wing creates lift, and this is how this large piece of metal can be lifted in the air so effortlessly.

The equation above simply says the faster air goes, the less pressure it has. The wing on any aircraft has a certain shape. The top part of the wing has more surface area than the bottom part of the wing. When the relative wind hits the leading edge of the wing, it is split.

Air goes above and below the wing.

With a larger surface area on top of the wing, the air must increase speed in order to meet the air as it converges on the back of the wing or trailing edge. This increase in speed lowers the pressure and the wing is lifted into this low-pressure area.

That's it, that's all it takes.

All we have to do now is add engines or thrust to push us forward to get that airflow over the wing and we can fly.

Here's a fun experiment the kids can try. Yes, you grown-up kids as well. Take a sheet of paper and cut it in half so it's about four inches wide and 11 inches long. Pinch one end of it so that the long end hangs down over the back of your hand. (see illustration) Now put your lips close to the paper and blow straight over the TOP of the paper. If you blow hard enough, you will see the paper lift up into your airstream.

You've just created lift!

There! Now you are all pilots! THE END!

Wellllll, OK, maybe we'll expand on these theories and look at how aviation works in a little more depth. (Even though you kids know it's magic that makes a plane fly, not some weird theory scientists had to invent because they stopped believing in magic.)

"Keep me clean so I fly fast!"

Drag

In order to fly through the air most efficiently, we must reduce the amount of drag on the aircraft. There are two types of drag. Parasite drag and induced drag. Parasite drag refers to objects sticking out of the aircraft, like antennae and landing gear. (Not some Stephen King creation attached to the airplane sucking the lift out of it.) These objects can really slow an airplane down. That's not cool, that's a drag!

It's fairly easy to combat this type of drag simply by reducing objects sticking out of the aircraft such as antennae and retracting the gear. Induced drag is a direct result of lift. What may not be obvious to most people is that the tail of an aircraft, the horizontal section, is basically an upside down wing. Lift is created on the bottom part of the tail in order to pull the tail down and keep the nose up. But even with this inverted lift we have created induced drag.

So the wing must create more lift in order to offset this inverted lift. If the tail gives us –10% for lift, the wing must create 110% for the sum of 100%. Aircraft are now being designed to have several lifting surfaces so that more of the plane is being used which can lead to a reduction in wing size and therefore a reduction in induced drag. Thousands of hours of wind tunnel testing ensure maximum efficiency.

Life Lesson

Drag holds an airplane back. What kind of drag is holding you back in life? Streamline your thoughts so you too can fly faster and more efficiently.

_____

_____

_____

_____

_____

_____

_____

_____

_____

_____

_____

Writing/Flying Quotes

Feathers shall raise men even as they do birds towards heaven :— That is by letters written with their quills.

— *Leonardo da Vinci*

Or like a poet woo the Moon,
Riding an armchair for my steed,
And with a flashing pen harpoon
Terrific metaphors of speed.

— *Roy Campbell,* The Festivals of Flight, *1930*

It isn't often that a writer of superlative skills knows enough about flying to write well about it.

— *Samuel Hynes, "A Teller of Tales Tells His Own,"*
in the New York Times**,** *7 September 1997*

Thousands of volumes have been written about aviation, but we do not automatically have thousands of true and special friends in their authors. That rare writer who comes alive on a page does it by giving of himself, by writing of meanings, and not just of fact or of things that have happened to him. The writers of flight who have done this are usually found together in a special section on private bookshelves.

— *Richard Bach, "The Pleasure of Their Company,"*
in Flying *magazine, April 1968.*

Continued on p. 11

"My engines push me through the sky!"

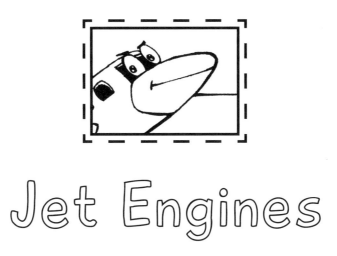

Jet Engines

There are four words that are always associated with how a jet engine operates.

Suck, squeeze, burn and blow.

The first step is air intake in the front of the engine, which is the sucking. This is followed by compression or squeezing. The compressors have a circular shape with many blades. You can see them by looking at the front of any jet engine. They are driven by a shaft connected to turbines in the exhaust or rear section.

The act of compressing air makes it very hot, which leads us to the third step, burn or combustion. Fuel nozzles then direct atomized fuel into the combustion chamber. This is mixed with the hot compressed air and ignited. The hot air exits the combustion chamber very rapidly, pushing the airplane forward. This is blow. This expelled air also flows over the turbines. Think of it as a windmill. As we stated before, the turbines are connected to the compressors at the front of the engine. The cycle is now complete by the forced air spinning the turbines; this keeps the compressors spinning, which in turn sucks in more air.

When the pilot pushes the power levers forward, he is adding more fuel to the fire. This results in an increase in temperature in the combustion chamber and therefore produces more thrust.

Some people don't like to fly on a turboprop aircraft because it has propellers. What they don't understand is that the turboprop engine is basically a jet engine. But instead of thrusting the air out of the back to propel the plane forward, it's thrust over a series of gears that spin a propeller, which in turn thrusts the airplane forward. Which type of design the engineers wish to use boils down to a matter of efficiency. As the technology advances, so do the engine designs. A propeller stops becoming efficient at a certain point. The max revolutions per minute must be kept at a speed where the tips of the propellers will not exceed the speed of sound. (Mach, or Mach 1. Mach 2 being twice the speed of sound, etc.)

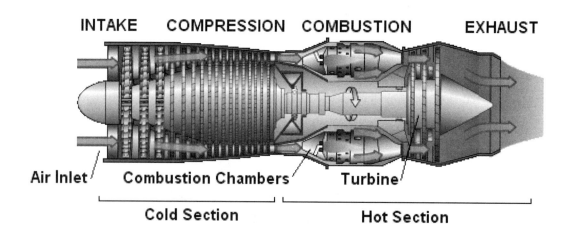

INTAKE   COMPRESSION   COMBUSTION   EXHAUST

Air Inlet   Combustion Chambers   Turbine

Cold Section   Hot Section

Continued from p. 7

The Progression of Flight

I was surprised at the silence and the absence of movement which our departure caused among the spectators, and believed them to be astonished and perhaps awed at the strange spectacle; they might well have reassured themselves. I was still gazing when M. Rozier cried to me—"You are doing nothing, and the balloon is scarcely rising a fathom."

"Pardon me," I answered, as I placed a bundle of straw upon the fire and slightly stirred it. Then I turned quickly but already we had passed out of sight of La Muette. Astonished I cast a glance towards the river. I perceived the confluence of the Oise. And naming the principal bends of the river by the places nearest them, I cried, "Passy, St. Germain, St. Denis, Sèvres!"

"If you look at the river in that fashion you will be likely to bathe in it soon," cried Rozier. "Some fire, my dear friend, some fire!"

> — *Marquis D'Arlandes, first flight of a hot air balloon, 21 November 1783*

Nothing will ever equal that moment of exhilaration which filled my whole being when I felt myself flying away from the earth. It was not mere pleasure; it was perfect bliss...

> — *Prof. Jacques Alexandre Cesare Charles, first free flight in a manned hydrogen balloon, December 1, 1783. Note: the exact adjective used by Prof. Charles to describe his emotions in French is not "exhilaration" but "hilarité," which can be translated as ecstasy, exhilaration, joy and/or excitement*

I cannot describe the delight, the wonder and intoxication, of this free diagonal movement onward and upward, or onward and downward....The birds have this sensation when they spread their wings and go tobogganing in curves and spirals through the sky.

> — *Alberto Santos-Dumont, first dirigible flight*

When once you have tasted flight, you will forever walk the earth with your eyes turned skyward, for there you have been, and there you will always long to return.

> — *This must be the most famous aviation quote that is **not** a verifiable quote. It is attributed everywhere (including some Smithsonian publications and the Washington Post newspaper) to Leonardo da Vinci, but no one has ever found a definitive source.*

Continued on p. 15

11

Writing/Flying Quotes

"I love flying high in the sky!"

Altitude

Why does the airplane fly so high?

There are two main reasons. One is fuel efficiency and the other is the weather. That's right! Bet you didn't think we were going to say that!
The higher you go in our atmosphere, the less dense the air becomes. When the air is less dense, jet engines are much more fuel efficient. Flying at 36,000 feet takes much less fuel than flying at 6,000 feet and the thinner air allows the aircraft to fly much faster due to less resistance.

You may also notice that when you fly easterly, the trip can take a lot quicker than if you're flying to the west. This is because of the jet stream.

> **jet stream**
> *noun*
> 1. a narrow, variable band of very strong, predominantly westerly air currents encircling the globe several miles above the earth. There are typically two or three jet streams in each of the northern and southern hemispheres.

The typical jet stream flows from west to east and travels at approx. 100 mph. It is usually between 5 to 9 miles up in the atmosphere. A pilot has access to many charts showing where the jet stream is on that particular day. It could actually have 90° curves in it to the north and south but will typically wind up flowing east again. Aircraft can climb up into the jet stream and depending on the time of year gain over hundred knots of airspeed just from the push of the wind. A pilot will search out the best altitude to give him/her the most efficient way to operate the aircraft. Be it in time savings or fuel savings.

Most large commercial aircraft fly high also to be above the weather. Most of the bad weather you see such as snow, rain or clouds will occur at altitudes up to 15,000 feet above the earth's surface.

One exception is thunderstorms, which can climb as high as 50,000 feet. An airliner will go around any thunderstorm in its path. Flying well above the weather keeps the aircraft out of any turbulence caused by most cloud formations. More on turbulence a bit later.

Continued from p. 11

THE WESTERN UNION TELEGRAPH COMPANY.
INCORPORATED
23,000 OFFICES IN AMERICA.   CABLE SERVICE TO ALL THE WORLD.

ROBERT C. CLOWRY, President and General Manager.

RECEIVED at

170

176 C KA C8 33 Paid,   Via Norfolk Va

Kitty Hawk N C Dec 17

Bishop M Wright

        7 Hawthorne St

Success four flights thursday morning all against twenty one mile

wind started from Level with engine power alone average speed

through air thirty one miles longest 57 seconds inform Press

home shown Christmas .   Orevelle Wright   525P

Success four flights Thursday morning all against twenty one mile wind started from Level with engine power alone average speed through air thirty one miles longest 57 seconds inform Press home Christmas.

> — *Orville Wright, 17 December 1903. This first telegraph home had two transcription errors. It should have read 59 seconds and Orville's name was spelled "Orevelle." Bishop Milton Wright received the telegram at about 5:30 p.m., and showed it to Katharine a few minutes later. Supper was delayed while the telegram was sent over to Lorin's home and the news was telegraphed to Octave Chanute*

With a short dash down the runway, the machine lifted into the air and was flying. It was only a flight of twelve seconds, and it was uncertain, wavy, creeping sort of flight at best; but it was a real flight at last and not a glide.

> — *Orville Wright, first flight of a heavier-than-air aircraft*

Those who understand the real significance of the conditions under which we worked will be surprised rather at the length than the shortness of the flights made with an unfamiliar machine after less than one minute's practice. The machine possesses greater capacity of being controlled than any of our former machines.

> — *Wilbur Wright*

Continued on p. 27

"My radar shows me the way around bad WX!"

Radar

Most modern aircraft have onboard radar. This is typically found in the nose of the plane. The radar dish will send out a signal, if that signal hits an object such as moisture, it will bounce the signal back to the radar dish.

Weather radar is used to detect the presence of thunderstorms. The onboard computers turn the returning signal into different colors on the radar screen to show the severity of the storm. Green on the scope is typically just rain, yellow is more severe and red would be a major thunderstorm.

Pilots are taught how to read the radar screen to understand the size and depth of the storm. Distance is calculated by the speed in which the signal returns to the aircraft. Obviously the longer it takes for the signal to return, the farther away the storm is. Most sophisticated onboard radar can be tilted up or down by the pilot. This allows the pilot to see how high the storm is and if he/she needs to take action.

If the radar is on and the radar screen stays blank, it's probably a sunny day. Trust the pilot. He/she has taken numerous meteorological classes and is very versed on radar and weather. Pilots make the flight as safe as possible even in bad weather.

"Crack!" "Rumble!"

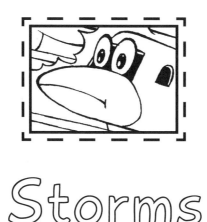

Storms

The sheer size of a thunderstorm can be staggering.

A line of thunderstorms can be several hundred miles long. A single thunderstorm can average fifteen miles across. Thunderstorms contain almost every major hazard known to flying: extremely heavy rain, hail, icing, large changes in wind direction, warm air rising and cold air falling.

Thunderstorms are the most hazardous type of weather an aircraft could encounter. The Federal Aviation Regulations and Airman's Information Manual has set guidelines about how near an aircraft should fly to a thunderstorm. With the sheer size of a thunderstorm even one over 100 miles away can appear as close as several miles. Don't worry, the captain can tell the distance with onboard radar and experience.

Lightning can often be seen coming out of the storms. While flying, lightning is not as dangerous as you think. Aircraft are designed so that lightning can pass through the airframe practically harmlessly. Although lightning is not totally harmless. It has been known to damage sensitive electrical equipment such as radios or on board navigation computers. If the crew suspects their aircraft has been hit by lightning, they will send the aircraft to maintenance for an inspection.

If you look out at the wing or tail, you will see small wicks sticking out of the trailing edges. These are static wicks.

Static wicks are attached to the trailing edge of most control surfaces. These wicks are designed to disperse any electrical or static charge that may build up.

Life Lesson

How do you handle life's storms? Set your own personal guidelines to steer clear from or navigate away from them.

_____

_____

_____

_____

_____

_____

_____

_____

_____

_____

_____

_____

_____

"Pot holes in the sky..."

Turbulence

Have you ever experienced a bumpy flight?

A bumpy flight is a normal experience. But it can seem scary! That's why the flight attendants tell you to buckle your seatbelt!

Commercial airline companies want their passengers to have a comfortable ride and the pilot will seek out the best altitude to avoid turbulence. It's about safety and comfort, and turbulence usually isn't as bad as it feels to you when you're a passenger.

Aircraft are designed and tested to withstand all types of turbulence. The specifications a pilot studies will list "maneuvering speeds." These are the speeds at which the aircraft has been tested to withstand damage due to turbulence. The speed will be different for different weights. The pilot can slow the plane down for its specific weight at that time and be confident that there will be no damage.

On a clear day, low altitude turbulence is usually created by convection.

Convection is when fluid motion is not generated by any external source but by density differences in the fluid due to temperature gradients. In natural convection, fluid surrounding a heat source receives heat, becomes less dense, and rises. The surrounding, cooler fluid then moves to replace it. This cooler fluid is then heated and the process continues, forming a convection current. It's a complex thought but a simple process that transfers heat energy from the bottom of the convection cell to top.

In aviation, convection forms ascending and descending columns of air.

The best way to decrease this type of turbulence is to decrease the aircraft's speed. The most common turbulence occurs in the cumulus cloud. The big white puffy ones you see on summer afternoon. A cumulus cloud has constant rising and sinking air and the warm moist air will rise higher and higher until it cools and the moisture is squeezed out. This cooler air then sinks lower and lower until it is warmed up again and the cycle continues.

Why then, you ask yourself, do we sometimes have turbulence at a high altitude on a beautifully clear day? The answer would be a change in wind speed. When wind speeds change within a certain distance, it is as if the air is piling up on itself. This makes waves and the result is turbulence. I like to think of it as potholes in the sky. This type of turbulence is very hard to detect. This is why the captain asks you to keep your seatbelt loosely fastened around you at all times!

Another type of turbulence is wake turbulence! It can be a surprising experience, both for crews and passengers, to encounter. And it's caused by other aircraft!

The autopilot holds the plane on course but not after what could be an uncomfortable loud thump and maybe a few degrees of bank. It usually only lasts a very brief amount of time and because it usually occurs in a quiet situation, passengers can be stressed by this unusual experience.

It's the control tower's job to make sure there is proper separation between aircraft taking off and landing. A landing aircraft that comes in to soon may encounter the turbulence created by an aircraft taking off or by the one landing in front of it. Lift over the wing of an aircraft can create wingtip vortices. These are spiraling columns of air that spin off the tip of the wing. If these vortices aren't given a long enough time interval to dissipate, they can send a smaller plane upside down. The tower will issue a warning to an aircraft on landing such as "747 heavy departing, caution, wake turbulence."

However, the responsibility of avoiding wake turbulence is transferred to the pilot when he/she accepts a transmission to "maintain a visual separation" or "fly a visual approach." Most airlines have rules about how the pilot will conduct the approach and landing phase of the flight.

Most wake turbulence accidents occurred during the approach phase of the flight and at very low altitude, usually less than 200 feet above the runway.

Approximately 90% of accidents involving wake turbulence involve smaller aircraft that weigh less than 30,000 pounds.

Trust your pilot. He/she has been trained to avoid wake turbulence.

Life Lesson

Sometimes the turbulence in our own lives is easily detected. But other times it can blindside you on a warm and sunny day. Fasten your seatbelt and just hang on; this small bit of turbulence in the flight of life will smooth out soon.

Continued from p. 15

The course of the flight up and down was exceedingly erratic, partly due to the irregularity of the air, and partly to lack of experience in handling this machine.

— *Orville Wright*

They done it! They done it! Damned if they ain't flew.

— *Johnny Moore, shouted while running to the village of Kitty Hawk. 17 December 1903.*

This machine was a failure to the extent that it could not fly. In other respects it was a very important and necessary stepping stone.

— *Igor Ivanovitch Sikorsky, regards the first helicopter, built 1909*

Both optimists and pessimists contribute to the society. The optimist invents the aeroplane, the pessimist the parachute.

— *George Bernard Shaw*

Suddenly, Santos-Dumont points the end of the machine skyward, and the wheels visibly, unambiguously, leave the soil: the aeroplane flies. The whole crowd is stirred. Santos-Dumont seems to fly like some immense bird in a fairy tale.

— *Le Figaro, first powered flight in public, 24 October 1906*

I thought I would keep it on the ground until I became familiar with it, but on account of the wind, I unexpectedly took to the air, and the first thing I knew, I was flying.

— *Arthur Pratt Warner, Beloit, Wisconsin. Warner was the first individual in the U.S. to purchase an aeroplane, a Curtiss biplane, that he assembled himself. He had only intended to taxi when he made what was Wisconsin's first flight, 4 November 1909*

I headed for this white mountain, but was caught in the wind and the mist . . . I followed the cliff from north to south, but the wind, against which I was fighting, got even stronger. A break in the coast appeared to my right, just before Dover Castle. I was madly happy. I headed for it. I rushed for it. I was above ground!

— *Louis Bleriot, first across the English Channel*

Continued on p. 31

"Pets are passengers, too. I keep them safe!"

Pets

People aren't the only ones who have to deal with a bit of turbulence during a flight.

Do you like to fly with Fluffy? As a pilot, you see quite a few pets coming on board, and over the years I've learned that there is a science to making sure your pet has a safe and comfortable flight.

Maybe you don't have a pet or haven't flown with one, but some people do! People carry little animals like small cats or dogs in carriers and place them under the seat! But if the animal is large, it has to go in the cargo hold.

When flying with pets, call and check with the airline you will be flying as early as possible. Different airlines have different restrictions and rules when it comes to flying with animals. Make your reservation as early as possible; some airlines will require a certificate from your veterinarian within the past 30 days that certifies your pet is in good health.

Pet carriers have to be secure! Some news reports have showed pets that escaped from flimsy carriers.

Numerous examples have been shown with pets that will damage teeth and have bleeding gums and mouths while trying to chew their way out of their cage. This is a form of anxiety.

Put your pet carrier out several days before your trip, put in blankets and favorite toys and all the things that your pet loves and allow the pet to get used to it and use it as a comfort zone. On the day you travel, put in an old T-shirt with your scent on it. Make sure the carrier is adequately ventilated. It's smart to use a carrier with an extra rim around it so their holes won't be covered if the cage is pressed up against the boxes! Let Fluffy breathe!

If your pet is nervous it's best to put them in the carrier several days before the flight and drive them to a noisy environment several times so they get used to additional noise around them!

It's very important to make sure your contact information is on your pet and on the carrier. Perhaps even several times repeatedly. Make sure your cell phone information is on your pet's collar. It won't do any good if they're calling a home number and nobody's home!

Some people give their pet medicine to make them sleepy. But that's not good! Contrary to popular belief it's best not to sedate your animal unless they are frantic. Altitude and cargo hold climates could act negatively with sedation medication! What if your dog slept so much that he missed his connection? Feed your pet 6 to 8 hours before the flight. Give your animal only a little water immediately before placing him or her in the carrier.

Millions of pets are flown with their owners each year. Call the airline, follow their rules and ask their advice. They've done it all before. Your pet is safe in the friendly skies!

Continued from p. 27

We are safely on the other side of the pond. The job is finished.

> — *Lieutenant Commander Albert Read, radio transmission after first transatlantic air crossing, 27 May 1919*

That's the best way to cross the Atlantic.

> — *Sir Arthur Whitten Brown, first nonstop across the Atlantic, upon landing 15 June 1919*

What? Only sixteen hours! Are you sure?

> — *Orville Wright, on hearing about the first nonstop flight across the Atlantic, 15 June 1919*

The hardships and perils of the past month were forgotten in the excitement of the present. We shook hands with one another, our hearts swelling with those emotions invoked by achievement and the glamour of the moment. It was, and will be, perhaps the supreme hour of our lives.

> — *Sir Ross Smith, K.B.E., first from London to Australia*

These phantoms speak with human voices … able to vanish or appear at will, to pass in and out through the walls of the fuselage as though no walls were there … familiar voices, conversing and advising on my flight, discussing problems of my navigation, reassuring me, giving me messages of importance unattainable in ordinary life.

> — *Charles Lindbergh, first solo across the Atlantic*

Where am I?

> — *Charles A. Lindbergh, upon arrival in Paris*

I'm Douglas Corrigan. Just got in from New York, where am I? … I intended to fly to California.

> — *'Wrong Way' Corrigan, upon arrival in Ireland after his unapproved solo transatlantic flight. He maintained he had 'compass troubles.'*

Where am I?

> *In Gallegher's pasture . . . have you come far?*

From America.

> — *Amelia Earhart, first solo flight by a woman across the Atlantic, upon arrival in an open field near Londonderry, Northern Ireland*

Continued on p. 35

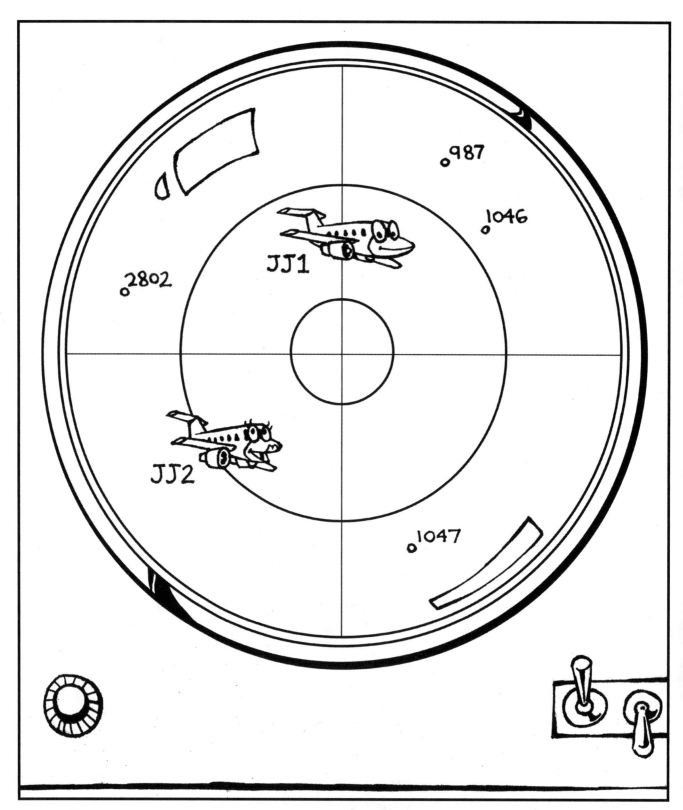

"My friends on the ground watch over me."

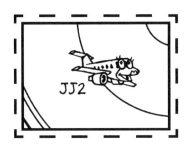

Air Traffic Control

Who directs traffic in the air? When your airplane flies into the airport, it's like a highway in the sky. Air-traffic control is an integral part of aviation.

There are several different departments that handle the aircraft as the flight progresses. A pilot sitting in his/her airplane will first call clearance. Clearance control issues the route that air traffic control wants the aircraft to fly. The larger commercial airliners that fly the same route every day can have their route sent via computer directly to the cockpit.

This can include the initial altitude, the final altitude, radar vectors, the series of fixes the aircraft must navigate to, and a transponder code, which is what air-traffic control will be able to track the aircraft by. This is a four-digit number that the pilot enters into a box called a transponder.

Once the pilot has his/her route he/she then calls ground control. Ground control is responsible for all movement at the airport. Ground control also talks to any automobiles or service trucks that are on the ramp area. Any vehicle moving on the airport must call ground control. Ground control will direct the pilot where to taxi to and what taxiways he/she must use to get there.

The pilot then contacts the tower. Tower control is responsible for flights in the immediate airport traffic area. Normally this area extends from the surface of the airport to 2,500 feet and out for approximately a 5-mile radius. The tower is who issues takeoff and landing clearances.

Once the pilot is in the air, the tower will tell the pilot to contact departure. Departure control usually has the aircraft under radar surveillance. Departure will advise the pilot to climb to a certain altitude. Departure will also start them heading toward their first navigational fix. Departure may handle an aircraft as much to 30 or 40 miles away from the airport after getting them on their course.

Departure will inform the pilot to contact center. Centers typically handle the high-altitude airspace. Depending on the length of the flight the pilot may talk sequentially to several different controllers at the same center and then get passed along to the next airspace that the following center controls.

At approximately 100 miles out from destination the center will start descending an aircraft. Center will bring them down to within approximately 40 miles of the airport and then hand the aircraft and pilot off to Approach Control. Approach Control will start lining up the aircraft for arrival to the airport. They will direct flights onto the final approach course and then hand them off to the tower. The tower is responsible for issuing the final landing clearance. Once the aircraft has landed and has taxied clear of the runway it is again guided by ground control back to its parking spot.

I was a passenger on the journey...just a passenger. Everything that was done to bring us across was done by Wilmer Stultz and Slim Gordon. Any praise I can give them they ought to have...I do not believe that women lack the stamina to do a solo trip across the Atlantic, but it would be a matter of learning the arts of flying by instruments only, an art which few men pilots know perfectly now...

> — *Amelia Earhart, first flight of a*
> *woman across the Atlantic*

Midway in Yokohama Bay we passed the volcano O Shima which was putting out great clouds of steam, and soon afterwards through a rift in the clouds we could see Japan's famous Fujiyama with the sun shining on its snow capped dome some 12,400 feet above sea level—a truly beautiful sight.

> — *Lt. Leslie Arnold,*
> *first around the world*

Somewhat to my dismay Everest bore that immense snow plume which means a mighty wind tearing across the summit, lifting clouds of powered snow and driving it with blizzard force eastward. Up went the machine into a sky of indescribable blue till we came on a level with the great peak itself, This astonishing picture of Everest, its plume now gradually lessening, its tremendous southern cliffs flanked by Makalu, was a sight which must remain in the mind all the years of one's life.

> — *Lt. Col. L. V. Stewart Blacker,*
> *first flight over Everest*

I happened to be the man on the spot, but any of the rest of the fellows would have done what I did.

> — *Jack Knight, first night mail flight, which was*
> *part of a record-setting transcontinental airmail relay*

Apart from a few tricky minutes in low cloud near the North Downs the journey over Folkestone and Boulogne down to Beauvais was uneventful but wet and hardly ever over 200 feet above ground . . . we eventually landed at Le Bourget at 10:15 a.m. In those days the airfield consisted of several canvas hangars, some wooden sheds and a lot of mud.

> — *Jerry Shaw, first flight of a*
> *paying passenger from England to France*

Continued on p. 43

Writing/Flying Quotes

"I always follow the rules to keep you safe!"

The FAA

While this chapter might seem a little dry, it's important to understand the FAA's role in keeping aviation safe.

According to Wikipedia, "The Federal Aviation Administration is the national aviation authority of the United States. An agency of the United States Department of Transportation, it has authority to regulate and oversee all aspects of American civil aviation. The Federal Aviation Act of 1958 created the organization under the name Federal Aviation Agency. The agency adopted its current name in 1966 and became a part of the U.S. Department of Transportation."

Basically, the FAA makes the rules and we pilots follow them!

The FAA's major functions include:

- Regulating U.S. commercial space transportation.

- Regulating air navigation facilities geometry and flight inspection standards.

- Encouraging and developing civil Aeronautics, including new aviation technology.

- Issuing, suspending or revoking pilot certificates.

- Regulating civil aviation to promote safety, especially through local offices called Flight Standards District Offices (FSDO).

- Developing and operating a system of air-traffic control and navigation for both civil and military aircraft.

- Researching and developing the national airspace system and civil aeronautics.

- Developing and carrying out programs to control aircraft noise and other environmental effects of civil aviation.

Reading through these roles we can see the overall goal is to advance aviation technology and safety.

The FAA is divided into four lines of businesses. Each line of business has a specific role within the FAA.

Airports—plans and develops projects involving airports, overseeing their construction and operations. Ensures compliance with federal regulations.

Air-traffic organization—primary duty is to safely and efficiently move air-traffic within the national airspace system. ATO employees manage air-traffic facilities including air-traffic control towers' terminal radar approach control facilities.

Aviation safety—responsible for aeronautical certification of personnel and aircraft, including pilots, airline stewards, and mechanics.

Commercial space transportation—ensures protection of U.S. assets during the launch or reentry of commercial space vehicles.

For years it was a federal regulation that all passengers must have their cell phones turned off for the whole flight. However on October 31, 2013, the FAA announced it would allow airlines to expand the passengers' use of portable electronic devices during all phases of flight. Unfortunately, this doesn't mean you can start calling all your friends as cell phone calls will still be prohibited. Implementation will vary among airlines so check before you fly.

Currently, devices must be held or put in the seat back pocket during the actual takeoff and landing. Cell phones must be in airplane mode or with cellular service disabled, with no signal bars displayed, and cannot be used for voice communications due to FCC regulations that prohibit any airborne calls using cell phones.

"Safety is always the right answer."

Safety and Security

Globally, there are security and safety standards by country and airline.

The safety of traveling on United States airlines has never been greater. This is due to the FAA's diligence in creating the federal aviation regulations and all airlines' willingness to maintain these rules. In the past 10 years there have been hundreds of millions of flights conducted inside the United States without a single major air catastrophe (2004-2014).

Every single department inside an aviation organization has one purpose—safety. From the men in the office running the business aspect, to the pilots, the flight attendants, the mechanics, the ground crew and anyone approaching the aircraft; safety is instilled in them.

There is no other form of transportation that is scrutinized or investigated and monitored as much as commercial aviation. Many statistics and figures prove that airline transportation is the safest way to travel.

This information relates to our logical, reasoning, rational mind. Worrying about safety is an emotion that seems to bypass those of logical thought. As with anything, knowledge is the key. Don't jump to fearful conclusions. It's very easy for those that do not fear to fly to quote statistics. But here's one for you anyway! Based on the airlines' incredible safety record, if you flew every day of your life, probability dictates that it would take you 19,000 years before you would have a fatal accident. That's one heckuva statistic!

Fear is one of our most powerful emotions.

Education is the best way to cure it.

Continued from p. 35

Even though the release was pulled, the rocket did not rise at first, but the flame came out, and there was a steady roar. After a number of seconds it rose, slowly until in cleared the frame, and then at express-train speed, curving over to the left, and striking the ice and snow, still going at a rapid rate. It looked almost magical as it rose, without any appreciably greater noise or flame, as if it said, "I've been here long enough; I think I'll be going somewhere else, if you don't mind."

— Robert Goddard, in regards to the first rocket flight using liquid propellants at Aunt Effie's farm 17 March 1926.

Rather routine.

— Frank Collbohm, Douglas Aircraft Company flight engineer, notation in the flight log during the first ever flight of the DC-3 Clover Field in Santa Monica, California, 17 December 1935

One has the feeling of enormous safety. You don't have the torque from the propeller. You have no noise; it's almost like little electric motors humming inside, and you feel sort of safe.

— Erich Warsitz, first flight of the Heinkel 178, reported in AOPA Pilot, *June 1992. This was the first jet powered aircraft. 27 August 1939.*

It's only the beginning but the implications are terrific.

— Gerald Sayer, first flight in the Gloster-Whittle E28 jet, 1941

It looked like a fiery sword going into the sky. There came this enormous roar and the whole sky seemed to vibrate; this kind of unearthly roaring was something human ears had never heard. It is very hard to describe what you feel when you stand on the threshold of a whole new era; of a whole new age. … It's like those people must have felt—Columbus or Magellan—that for the first time saw entire new worlds and knew the world would never be the same after this. … We knew the space age had begun.

— Dr. Walter Robert Dornberger, regards the first successful flight of the A-4 rocket, to the edge of space, 3 October 1942

Continued on p. 47

*"I hold plenty of air inside me so
you can breathe easy!"*

Inside the Plane

Aircraft cabins are pressurized to create a safe and comfortable environment for passengers and crew. When flying at high altitudes, conditioned air is pumped into the cabin. This is called bleed air. It is typically air that is bled off of the engines at the compressor stage.

The air is cooled, humidified, if necessary mixed with recirculated air and then distributed to the cabin by the environmental control systems. Located somewhere in the cabin is the outflow valve. If the pressure gets too great inside the cabin the outflow valve will automatically open to release some of the pressure. Different aircraft are pressurized to different levels.

Typically a commercial airliner cruising at 36,000 feet will have a cabin pressure of approximately 8,000 feet above sea level. Smaller corporate jets may only have a cabin pressure of 4,000 feet.

Today's airliners are designed so that even if one engine is disabled, the remaining engine has enough power and additional bleed air to compensate. Again, safety is the developing factor. Pressurization helps to protect crew and passengers from the risk of a number of physiological problems caused by low outside air pressure.

It's important to always listen to the flight attendants as they go over the safety features of the aircraft. Educating yourself in areas such as hypoxia, altitude sickness, decompression sickness and barotrauma will give you an understanding of why pressurization is necessary.

Partial pressurization of cargo holds is required to prevent damage to pressure sensitive goods that might expand, leak or burst and which can be crushed on repressurization.

Continued from p. 43

For the first time I was flying by jet propulsion. No engine vibrations. No torque and no lashing sound of the propeller. Accompanied by a whistling sound, my jet shot through the air. Later when asked what it felt like, I said, "It felt as though angels were pushing".

> — *Generalleutnant Adolf Galland,*
> *on his first flight in a jet,*
> *the Messerschmitt 262, May 1943*

At 42,000' in approximately level flight, a third cylinder was turned on. Acceleration was rapid and speed increased to .98 Mach. The needle of the machmeter fluctuated at this reading momentarily, then passed off the scale. Assuming that the off-scale reading remained linear, it is estimated that 1.05 Mach was attained at this time.

> — *(Then) Captain Charles E. Yeager, Air Corps, formal typewritten*
> *test flight report on first supersonic flight, 14 October 1947.*
> *NACA tracking data and the XS-1's own oscillograph instrumentation later*
> *showed 'Glamorous Glennis' had attained Mach 1.06 at about 43,000 feet*

Leveling off at 42,000 feet, I had thirty percent of my fuel, so I turned on rocket chamber three and immediately reached .96 Mach. I noticed that the faster I got, the smoother the ride. Suddenly the Mach needle began to fluctuate. It went up to .965 Mach—then tipped right off the scale. … We were flying supersonic. And it was a smooth as a baby's bottom; Grandma could be sitting up there sipping lemonade.

> — *General Charles 'Chuck' Yeager, in regards to first supersonic flight*

Hey Ridley, that Machometer is acting screwy. It just went off the scale on me.

> — *General Charles 'Chuck' Yeager, first radio transmission after going*
> *supersonic for the first time, a coded message indicating success, 1947.*

As we went through mach one, the nose started dropping, so we just cranked that horizontal stabilizer down to keep the nose up. We got it above mach one, and once we got it above the speed of sound, then you have supersonic flow over the whole airplane, so you have no more shock waves on it that are causing buffeting...You really don't think about the

Continued on p. 51

"I try to stay quiet when I'm low to the ground."

Airports

Most large airports have what is known as noise abatement procedures. These are designed to reduce the impact of aircraft noise has on the community. These can be general for the whole airport or noise specific per individual runway. It depends on the population that may be on the departure and or approach end of that runway. Airliners will try to climb as quickly as possible to reach a certain altitude and then power back on the throttles to reduce the noise level.

Some airports have installed equipment that can measure the decibels the aircraft is putting off and for how long the aircraft is reaching a certain decibel level. An airport may fine an aircraft if it finds it to be breaking the max decibel level on a regular basis. The fine can be as much as $10,000 per incident.

Procedures have been put in place and are part of a runway use program and participation by pilots that is part regulation and part voluntary. Again, while safety is paramount to all air-traffic operations, noise sensitivity to the surrounding communities is also of key importance. Looking back at our FAA, one of its primary functions is to determine under what conditions flight operations may be conducted without undermining flight safety.

The decibel measuring equipment used by some airports has started to weigh both evening and late night noise more heavily. New routes are being designed that will have an aircraft approach an airport in a way that will minimize noise.

This program tries to maximize flights overwater and minimize flights over land whenever possible especially between the hours of 1 a.m. and 6 a.m. New routes using GPS waypoints are also being implemented. Each point will have a certain step down or a certain altitude at which the aircraft must be when reaching that point. They are being designed so

that an airliner can start its descent, power back on its throttles and practically coast all the way to the airport with the throttles at a low power setting, which correlates to a low noise setting. (And saves fuel as well!)

outcome of any kind of a flight, whether it's combat, or any other kinds of flights, because you really have no control over it... You concentrate on what you are doing, to do the best job you can, to stay out of serious situations. And that's the way the X-1 was.

> — *General Charles 'Chuck' Yeager, regards the first supersoninc flight, interview, 1 February 1991*

I wanted to go back for another 50 missions, but they ruled it out because I had a case of malaria that kept recurring. So I had to stay in the States and teach combat flying. I was shot down by a mosquito!

> — *Frank Hurlbut, P-38 pilot*

Your seat pushed you firmly in the back. Even then there is none of the shuddering brazen bellow of the high-powered piston engine. … Combined with a seemingly uncanny lack of vibration, this gives the impression almost of sailing through space, the engines with their glinting propeller discs utterly remote from the quiet security of this cabin.

> — *Derek Harvey, first turboprop airliner (Vickers-Armstrong Viscount)*

The drooping grandmothers, the crying babies, the continuous, raucous, unintelligible squawk of the loudspeaker, the constant push and jostle of new arrivals … make bus terminals look like luxury … Almost all U.S. airports are utterly barren of things to do. The dirty little lunch counters are always choked with permanent sitters staring at their indigestible food. … The traveler consigned to hours of tedious waiting can only clear a spot on the floor and sit on his baggage and, while oversmoking, drearily contemplate his sins.

> —Fortune *magazine, 1946*

Millions wonder what it is like to travel in the Comet at 500 miles an hour eight miles above the earth. Paradoxically there is a sensation of being poised motionless in space. Because of the great height the scene below scarcely appears to move; because of the stability of the atmosphere the aircraft remains rock-steady . . . One arrives over distant landmarks in an incredibly short time but without the sense of having traveled. Speed does not enter into the picture. One doubts one's wristwatch.

> — *C. Martin Sharp, first jet airliner (the de Havilland Comet 1)*

Continued on p. 59

"I stop quickly so my friends
can use the runway, too!"

Landing

Most commercial airliners' wheels touchdown while the aircraft is doing approximately a 140 miles an hour. A pilot will usually need to apply reverse thrust to slow the aircraft. Reverse thrust is basically taking the thrust that is pushing the aircraft forward and redirecting it forward to slow the aircraft down. This forward deflection of the exhaust is what results in the increase in noise level inside the cabin.

The pilot also applies pressure to the top of the rudder pedals with his feet. These are the aircraft's brakes. The pilot's goal is to slow the aircraft as quickly and safely as possible in order to exit the runway. An aircraft cannot legally touchdown while another aircraft is occupying the runway. In order to maintain a smooth flow of traffic, the pilot tries to exit the runway as quickly as possible to make way for the next incoming aircraft. Of course safety takes precedence. If the pilot needs to use more runway, he will. Obviously the length of a runway will also play a deciding factor in how much reverse thrust and breaking the pilot will need.

Trust your pilot. Chances are he/she has landed at that airport and on that particular runway numerous times and in numerous weather conditions.

"We all work together to keep you safe."

Training

The amount of training a pilot goes through to fly for a commercial airline or a corporation in the private sector is incredible. There are many steps involved.

Becoming a professional pilot involves obtaining several different licenses. Each license grants an increasing amount of flight privileges and responsibilities.

The standard order of the list is first of all becoming a private pilot, then obtaining a commercial pilots rating, followed by an instrument rating that will allow you to fly in the clouds. This is followed by a multi-engine rating and finally an airline transport pilot rating.

The airline transport pilot rating or license is as good as it gets. All of your pilots sitting up front have acquired this license. This could be considered the doctorate of aviation.

To give you an example of what it takes to obtain a private pilot's license, here is what the federal aviation regulations say:

> "A person who applies for a private pilot certificate must receive by law ground and flight training from an authorized instructor on the areas of operation of this section that apply to the aircraft category

and class ratings sought. There is a minimum of 40 hours flight time required to become a private pilot. The person seeking the private pilot certificate will be tested on preflight preparation, preflight procedures, airport base operations, takeoffs, landings, and 'go arounds,' performance maneuvers, ground reference maneuvers, navigation, slow flight stalls, basic instrument maneuvers, emergency operations, nine operations, and post flight procedures."

In addition to the aforementioned items, the pilot attempting to gain a private pilot license must also take classes in aerodynamics, federal Aviation Regulations, meteorology, radio communications, etc. (Remember, this is just to obtain a private pilot's license.)

But don't let this detour you from your dream of flying an airplane. The courses are laid out in a way that you can methodically follow and achieve your goals.

Every license will involve flying with an official from the Federal Aviation Administration or designated flight examiner who has been authorized by the FAA. Every flight test is preceded by an oral exam which can last up to 1 to 2 hours and most licenses require a written exam that a pilot must obtain a grade of 80 or better.

Typically professional pilots enjoy learning new things. They are in a constant mode of training or learning. Professional pilots will attend some form of recurrent training every six months or every year, depending on their ranking. A pilot's training never ends. Most recurrent training now takes place in some form of high-level simulator. The simulators are practically identical to the real aircraft.

When obtaining a type rating in a certain aircraft, the pilot only needs to complete the training in a high-level simulator and is then eligible to step into the aircraft and fly it. This simulator training is coupled with several weeks of ground school so the pilot is proficient in all areas.

The level-D simulators are large cockpits on hydraulic stilts. The hydraulics simulate the actual movement of an aircraft, whether it be climbing descending banking or even turbulence.

In some ways the simulator is superior in training to the actual aircraft. Technology has coupled computers to the simulators that can simulate any area of flight. Most importantly, they can simulate any emergency that can be conceived.

The pilot is repeatedly trained on engine fires, loss of engine, windshear, loss of hydraulics, failure of landing gear, and any other situation. If an emergency ever occurs in the air, rest assured the pilot has most likely seen the same situation in the simulator and has been over and over the proper procedures. Step-by-step checklists are kept in the simulator and in the cockpit of the aircraft to make sure all the steps involved in securing the emergency are taken.

Just like aircraft have scheduled maintenance, so do pilots. It's in the company's best interest to have healthy pilots. The Federal Aviation Regulations are very strict about aviation medicals. An airline pilot must have a medical evaluation every six months. Pilots' eyes and ears are checked and they are given a standard medical. Once pilots reach 35 years of age, they must have an EKG done to make sure their heart is healthy. The results are sent directly to Oklahoma City to the FAA headquarters. There, if the pilot's

heart is normal he/she may continue with his/her career. Once a pilot reaches 40 years of age he/she must have an EKG performed every year from then on.

Most pilots take it upon themselves to remain healthy. The ideal life includes focusing on eating right, working out, and making sure you are strong and have a healthy mind. Fitness also includes your brain, so don't forget to always read and learn and grow!

And here's another fun fact! Roughly half of all pilots are left-handed. This is the same percentage as left-handed presidents of the United States.

Continued from p. 51

Poyekhali.
(*translation*: Let's Go!)

> — *Yuri A. Gagarin, shouted as Vostok 1 lifted off, 12 April 1961*

I saw for the first time the earth's shape. I could easily see the shores of continents, islands, great rivers, folds of the terrain, large bodies of water. The horizon is dark blue, smoothly turning to black … the feelings which filled me I can express with one word—joy.

> — *Yuri A. Gagarin*

You're on your way, Jose!

> — *Deke Slayton, at Mission Control, to Alan Shepard at liftoff of Freedom 7, first American in space, 5 May 1961*

The first flight was relatively uneventful. Just one emergency, and another minor problem. A canopy-unsafe light illuminated at Mach 1.2 on the way to 1.5 at 50,000 feet, and later, during a fly-by requested by Johnson, fuel siphoning occurred. Not bad, as initial test flights go.

> — *Robert J, Gilliland, regards the first flight of the SR-71 Blackbird, 22 December 1964*

Pilot Jack Waddell eased throttles forward; Co-Pilot Brian Wygle called out speeds as a gentle giant of the air began to move; Flight Engineer Jess Wallick kept eyes glued to the gauges. The Boeing Model 747 Superjet gathered speed. The nose lifted. After 4,300 ft—less than half the 9,000 ft runway—main gear of the plane left the concrete. At 11:34 a.m., with a speed of 164 miles an hour, quietly and almost serenely, the age of spacious jets began.

> — *Boeing Magazine, first flight of the B-747*

The powered flight took a total of about eight and a half minutes. It seemed to me it had gone by in a lash. We had gone from sitting still on the launch pad at the Kennedy Space Center to traveling at 17,500 miles an hour in that eight and a half minutes. It is still mind-boggling to me. I recall making some statement on the air-to-ground radio for the benefit of my fellow astronauts, who had also been in the program a long time, that it was well worth the wait.

> — *Bob Crippen, regards first flight of the Space Shuttle, STS-1*

Continued on p. 63

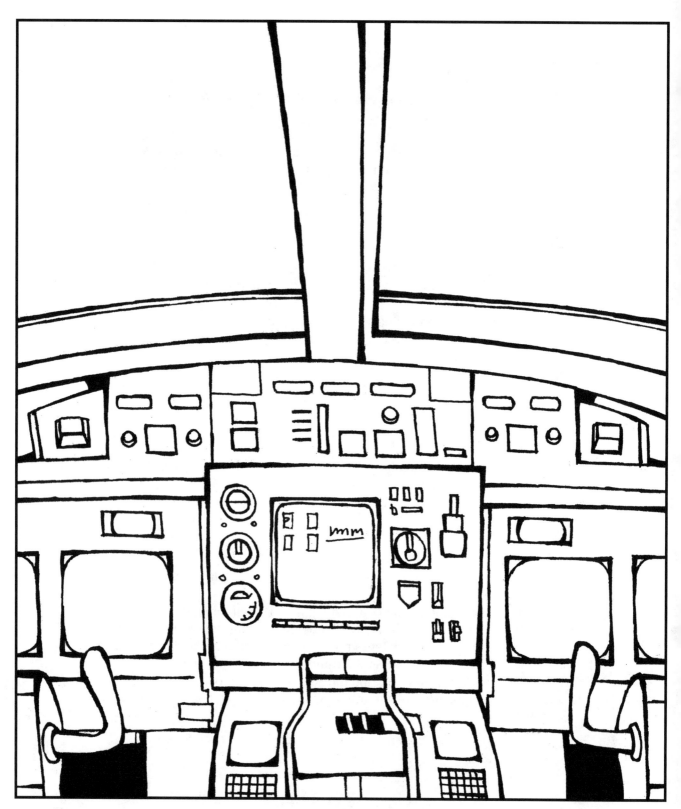

"All my technology is used to keep you safe."

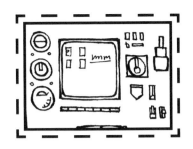

Inside the Cockpit

In today's modern world of aviation the avionics in today's airliners are a dazzling array of digital displays. The primary flight displays are built around an LCD or CRT display device.

The older analog instruments (what we refer to as steam gauges) are now combined on one compact display. This simplifies the pilot workflow and streamlines the cockpit layout. Being computer-driven and digital, a lot more information has been added in the smaller areas. Because safety is always at the forefront, mechanical gauges have not been completely eliminated from the cockpit. They often remain for backup purposes in the event of total electrical failure.

Smaller displays have their own battery source that can also be used if there is total electrical failure to the other components. These digital displays are now known as glass cockpits. The panels in front of the pilots are known as PFDs which stands for Primary Flight Display. There's typically one or two in the center of the firewall (the dashboard) that are known as MFD's or Multifunction Displays. Every display has some form of redundant display in the cockpit. Again this is due to safety.

Automated voices are now integrated into this equipment as well.

That means there's an electronic voice talking to the pilot inside the cockpit!

TCAS or Terminal Collision Avoidance Systems are installed in aircraft now. This is a display that will show aircraft near your position. They also show the altitude of the aircraft in relation to yours. If an aircraft gets too close, the color will change on the screen and if the computers calculate the aircraft are on a possible collision course they will offer a "resolution advisory" in the form of a voice saying to climb or descend. These do not happen often but when they do the pilot should follow the advice of the computer immediately.

The design and layout of the cockpit can seem very complex. Again, training is what it takes to understand that there is an actual flow to the layout. It's like being a baker in a restaurant and making dessert. The baker has trained for years, and knows just how to do it! Everyone in each profession has trained to have their skills. No matter what you do, make sure you do it well as stay focused, and healthy and strong.

Continued from p. 59

The dream is alive.

— John Young, after landing the first
Space Shuttle STS-1 at Edwards, 14 April 1981

Edwards Tower, this is Voyager One. We're ready to go.

Roger, Voyager One. You're cleared for takeoff. ATC clears Voyager One from Edwards Air Force Base to Edwards Air Force Base via flight plan route. Maintain 8,000. Godspeed.

— First around the world nonstop and nonrefueled. Dick Rutan and ATC

Our A320 behaved even better than expected—it is both delightfully responsive and reassuringly stable to fly, qualities which fly-by-wire brings together for the first time in an airliner. Never before have we enjoyed a first flight so much, and we are confident that airline pilots will feel the same way.

— Pierre Baud, first flight of a fully fly-by-wire airliner.
(Fly-by-wire definition: a system that replaces the conventional manual
flight controls of an aircraft with an electronic interface.)

The way the public sees it is this. If we don't leave, we are idiots. If we do leave but don't succeed in our mission, we are incompetent. But if we do succeed, it's because it was easy and anyone could have done it.

— Bertrand Piccard, first to balloon around the world, 1999

I am with the angels and just completely happy.

— Bertrand Piccard, Swiss pilot of the Breitling Orbiter 3,
first to balloon around the world, 20 March 1999

I am going to have a cup of tea, like any good Englishman.

— Brian Jones, British pilot of the Breitling Orbiter 3, first to balloon around
the world, in regards to what he is going to do next, 20 March 1999

I feel good.

— Yang Liwei, first Chinese astronaut in space, in his first report
from space, 34 minutes after the launch. 15 October 2003.
Reported by the Xinhua News Agency

Continued on p. 67

"I talk to the satellites in outer space.
They show me where to go!"

Navigation

How does a pilot know where to go?

Navigation of an aircraft has become simpler with the invention of GPS or the global positioning system. This is a satellite-based navigation system that was originally made up of a network of 24 satellites that were placed in orbit by the U.S. Department of Defense. In the 1980s the U.S. government allowed GPS to be used by civilians. Currently satellite data is free and will work anywhere in the world.

There are now at least 31 satellites in outer space and several more that have been decommissioned but can be reactivated if needed. Some would say the nostalgia of aviation has been changed with GPS. Pilots no longer need to rely on maps, dead reckoning or visual references to navigate from point A to point B. But again, safety is the overlying issue. Any aircraft equipped with GPS is in communication with at least four of the satellites in space at any given time. If the GPS system is being used to fly an approach into an airport, land-based equipment and more satellites are used. If at any given time there are fewer than four satellites sending information to the aircraft, the pilot will get a message informing him/her of this. Once again, there are backup systems to the GPS system should it fail.

Course tracking and recording devices are two examples of information that the GPS computers help in commercial aviation applications.

Life Lesson

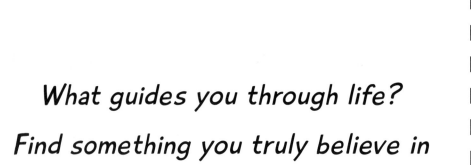

What guides you through life?
Find something you truly believe in
and let it help you track your
personal course.

Continued from p. 63

It was a mind-blowing experience, it really was—absolutely an awesome thing. … As I got to the top I released a bag of M&Ms in the cockpit. It was amazing . .. Looking out that window, seeing the white clouds in the LA Basin, it looked like snow on the ground.

> — *Mike Melvill, first to fly into space in a private aircraft, 21 June 2004*

It was absolutely perfect. You can handle this large aircraft as you can handle a bicycle.

> — *Jacques Rosay, test pilot, in regard to the A-380 first flight, 28 April 2005*

I showed it is possible to fly a little bit like a bird.

> — *Yves Rossy, first person to cross the English Channel strapped to a jet-powered wing. The 22 mile journey took 13 minutes. 26 September 2008*

We learned more about this airplane in the first 10 minutes of flying than we have in the last 100 days.

> — *Michael H. Carriker, test pilot, first flight of the Boeing 787, Boeing Field, 15 December 2009*

The airplane flew beautifully. There were no surprises.

> — *Randall L. Neville, test pilot, first flight of the Boeing 787, Boeing Field. As a highly experienced test pilot and former director of Flight Operations for the U.S. Air Force Test Pilot School, Neville knows the wonder of "no surprises" on a first flight. 15 December 2009.*

Totally uneventful. It was a very successful first flight. To be honest, it was a little bit boring.

> — *Fernando Alonso, Airbus Senior VP, head of the flight & integration center, and test engineer on the first flight of the A350 XWB. 14 June 2013*

New York to Tokyo could be less than an hour. You could be traveling at 19,000 miles per hour orbitally. After we've done the space program, we will be producing supersonic planes, which will go far, far, faster than Concorde.

> — *Richard Branson, CEO Virgin Atlantic & Virgin Galatic*

Continued on p. 73

"I get regular checkups to keep me
healthy and strong."

Flight Maintenance

The airplane is one of the safest vehicles on the planet.

The amount of regulation pertaining to aircraft maintenance is staggering. Much more than a car! Each type of aircraft has a set scheduled maintenance plan. When an aircraft flies for a certain number of hours, let's say 200 hours, it must go in for a routine checkup. (Different aircraft have different time intervals.)

The scheduled maintenance plans then increase. When an aircraft flies an additional 200 hours the same check might be performed. However, when it flies for a further 200 hours, bringing the total to 600 hours, a more extensive check is performed. Then when an aircraft flies a total of 1,200 hours an even more extensive check may be done.

Finally there may be a time, let's say, at approximately 4,000 hours, when the whole aircraft and engines must be overhauled. Even if the aircraft does not fly, there are certain parts that have a calendar life limit and must be changed out. You could be sitting in an aircraft that is 20 years old and yet if it just came out of this final inspection it can be considered like-new.

So just like Mom or Dad take the car in to get it maintained, or change the tires, aircraft are the same way too.

"I fly on invisible highways in the sky."

Aircraft Routes

Aircraft typically fly on assigned jet airways. I call these invisible highways in the sky.

In the old days aircraft had only VOR's (VHF Omni-directional Range network) to navigate to. Since the 1960s the VOR network has been the backbone of America's aviation navigation system.

The VHF Omni-directional Range network is a land-based system. Each VOR emits a signal on a certain frequency that a pilot can navigate to and from on any of the 360° bearings or radials surrounding the equipment. With the introduction of GPS, the systems, although they have upheld the national airspace system for over half a century, are becoming obsolete.

When GPS was first implemented, it was possible to take off from an airport, put in the identifier of the airport you wish to fly to and fly directly to it. So as not to compromise safety, a series of highways with certain waypoints has been designed. Air-traffic control procedures and air-traffic congestion typically prevent aircraft from flying directly to their destinations.

These waypoints typically marked the beginning of a standard terminal arrival route (STAR). These waypoints would be where approach control sends an aircraft to the initial point. This forms a line of aircraft heading for the same airport or airports in the vicinity.

The aircraft's flight management system (FMS) is uploaded with thousands of different airways. When the pilot receives his/her clearance, he/she is given his/her route which is then programmed into the FMS. The aircraft can then follow this route precisely using GPS. In 2002, the system was deemed so reliable that between 29,000 feet and 41,000 feet the 2,000-foot vertical separation minimum separating aircraft was reduced to 1,000 feet.

If you look out the window sometimes you might be surprised by how close an aircraft looks. This is called reduced vertical separation minimums (RVSM). The onboard equipment can hold an aircraft so precisely that aircraft can be within 1,000 feet of each other and remain safe. This act alone greatly reduced congestion in the sky, as we could then fit twice as many aircraft in this airspace safely.

Other forms of invisible waypoints are used near airports if the airport is congested or if the weather is too poor to land. These are called holding patterns. They are depicted on the aircraft's navigation usually with one starting point and the direction in which the aircraft should turn. Holding patterns have certain speed limits depending on the altitude such as: an airliner holding above 14,000 feet would be flown at 265 knots. From 6,001 feet to 14,000 feet, the speed is 230 knots and the speed from a minimum height up to 6,000 feet would be 200 knots. An airliner can ask for 10-mile legs so that it is flying straight and level more often than turning. There can be several aircraft in a holding pattern at the same time, obviously each at a different altitude. The pilot is given a time in which he/she may expect to be released from the holding pattern. A pilot will evaluate the amount of fuel onboard and may decide to stay in a holding pattern at an airport for a while or possibly continue on to the alternate airport listed on the flight plan.

Continued from p. 67

There's a real opportunity to have a vertical takeoff and landing electric supersonic jet.

— Elon Musk. If anybody else said it, it's crazy talk. For the founder of Paypal, Solar City, Tesla and Space X it's something to work on. TV interview with Stephen Colbert, *24 July 2014*

A drug seductive to even the fiercest Luddite, GPS makes skill, knowledge and intuition obsolete. It makes us at once infants and gods. Observer and observed, we watch from on high as our icon, a digital metaphor of self-awareness, creeps across the map. With GPS, there is no longer such a thing as "lost." Navigation, a great and noble art whose traditions stretch back into prehistory, has been replaced by a computer game. Its tools, the products of so much experience, ingenuity and self-sacrifice, will soon become curiosities; its methods and skills, so recently separating life and death, will eventually be forgotten.

— Peter Garrison, contributing editor, Flying *magazine, The Importance of Being Lost: We Lost Something When We Lost "Lost," July 2014.*

I'm a doctor not a pilot, Jim!

— Dr. Leonard (Bones) McCoy, Star Trek USS Enterprise

(Stardate Unknown)
Flying an aeroplane with only a single propeller to keep you in the air. Can you imagine that?

— Captain Picard, from Star Trek: The Next Generation USS Enterprise

Buttons . . . check. Dials . . . check. Switches . . . check. Little colored lights . . . check.

— The Bill Waterson comic character Calvin, of 'Calvin and Hobbes' fame

When it comes to testing new aircraft or determining maximum performance, pilots like to talk about "pushing the envelope." They're talking about a two dimensional model: the bottom is zero altitude, the ground; the left is zero speed; the top is max altitude; and the right,

Continued on p. 83

"Teamwork is VERY important."

Teamwork

Have you ever had to be part of a team? Sports teams or a team of friends working together on a school project can work to create something amazing! In life, teamwork is very important.

It takes an amazing amount of teamwork to make an airline run. Cockpit resource management (CRM) was developed primarily for improving air safety. It focused on interpersonal communication, leadership and decision-making in the cockpit. Later the term was generalized to crew resource management as airlines realized the need to include all flight personnel, not just the cockpit. Since the 1990s this has become a global standard. As we've stressed before everything in aviation boils down to safety.

Studies have shown that by both groups, pilots and flight attendants, using CRM together communication barriers were reduced and problems could be solved more efficiently. There are now a wide range of activities where people who must make dangerous time-critical decisions are studying CRM models to improve their own safety levels. Areas can include air-traffic control, firefighting, medical operating rooms, and ship handling.

"Your trip starts long before you get on the airplane.
Be patient and know the rules."

Airports and Security

Your flight begins well before you even get to the airport.

With today's aviation, safety and security is paramount. Know the rules before you go and plan for them. This will make it a much more relaxing and enjoyable trip. If you're traveling with children, explain the check-in and security procedures ahead of time. In larger airports or heavy traffic times of day, give yourself enough room to get to the airport, check in, and go through security to have a little relaxation time. In today's modern airports, there's lots to do and see. Some airports now have world-class chefs opening restaurants. Massages are even available in some terminals. Just don't fall asleep and miss your flight!

To expedite your time in line, the U.S. government is now offering security precheck. Check the government websites to see where an airport security precheck office is located near you and what you will need if you decide to become a security prechecked passenger.

As with anything in life, for an enjoyable trip, be prepared and know the rules.

"The flight attendants go through lots of training too.
Listen to them and they will help you."

The Flight Crew

On a commercial flight, the flight attendant is a highly trained individual who is well equipped to manage passenger needs!

Flight attendants are on board to help you, not just serve you. They have also gone through extensive training on aircraft knowledge. They are well-versed in emergency procedures. They have been trained and go through additional trainings each year on how to properly use the emergency exits, slides, and the rafts on board. They know what they're doing—listen to them. It's against the law to disobey a crew member's command.

You'll have a much more enjoyable trip if you sit back and listen to the experts. And did you know that flight attendants are highly trained in emergency care? They know how to operate basic onboard medical kits, and how to respond in a crisis. Passengers' actions can be unexpected sometimes! Flight attendants have broken up fist fights in the air, performed CPR on passengers, and even delivered babies!

"Spread your wings and reach for your goals!"

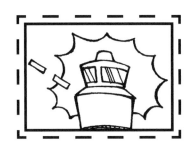

Careers in Aviation

Pilot and flight attendant are just two careers in aviation. There are many other positions!

Are you good at talking to people? Maybe a career in sales is what you need. Are you friendly and you love to work at an airport? Maybe a baggage carrier, or an air traffic control employee, or even an airplane mechanic would be the job for you.

If you are not sure if you are cut out to be a pilot or a flight attendant there are many jobs in the airline industry that can be fun and rewarding. There are thousands of people behind the scenes and in offices to ensure that planes and airlines run properly and efficiently.

A business college degree with an emphasis on aviation will give you a leg up in this area. Are you mechanical? Aviation mechanics perform a very important role in aviation. It's up to them to keep the aircraft in perfect flying condition. Mechanics take great pride in signing off an aircraft to be airworthy again.

Do you love being around airports? Maybe being a gate agent is right for you. Enjoy being outside? The people working on the ramp are the ones responsible for bringing the aircraft in and out of the terminal areas.

This is true in commercial and corporate aviation. Corporate aviation also offers huge opportunities. I have found aviation to be a rewarding career. If your kids have a love of flying, encourage them to spread their own wings and reach for whatever goals they desire. We like to say Desire, Discipline and Dedication. If you combine these three things in anything you do, you will succeed. Go ahead, live your dream career in the airline or aviation industry!

Continued from p. 73

maximum velocity, of course. So, the pilots are pushing that upper-right-hand corner of the envelope. What everybody tries not to dwell on is that that's where the postage gets canceled, too.

— Admiral Rick Hunter, U.S. Navy

Death is just nature's way of telling you to watch your airspeed.

— Anon.

For years politicians have promised the Moon. I'm the first one to be able to deliver it.

— Richard Nixon, 1969

WHY I WANT TO BE A PILOT

When I grow up I want to be a pilot because it's a fun job and easy to do. That's why there are so many pilots flying around these days.

Pilots don't need much school. They just have to learn to read numbers so they can read their instruments.

I guess they should be able to read a road map, too.

Pilots should be brave to they won't get scared it it's foggy and they can't see, or if a wing or motor falls off.

Pilots have to have good eyes to see through the clouds, and they can't be afraid of thunder or lightning because they are much closer to them than we are.

The salary pilots make is another thing I like. They make more money than they know what to do with. This is because most people think that flying a plane is dangerous, except pilots don't because they know how easy it is.

I hope I don't get airsick because I get carsick and if I get airsick, I couldn't be a pilot and then I would have to go to work.

— Purported to have been written by a fifth-grade student at Jefferson School, Beaufort, SC. It was first published in the South Carolina Aviation News.

Arguing with a pilot is like wrestling with a pig in the mud, after a while you begin to think the pig likes it.

— Seen on a General Dynamics bulletin board. It was Mark Twain who said, "Never try and teach a pig to sing. It's a waste of your time, and it annoys the pig."

Continued on p. 86

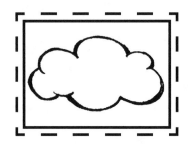

Letter to the Reader

I wanted to make flying fun again. That's the reason I've written this book. I was 17 years old when I flew an airplane by myself for the first time. It was my first solo. I remember taking off from the airport in Nashua, NH. After "circling the pattern" a couple times with my instructor (that is, we take off and follow a rectangular pattern around the airport to come in and land again), he instructed me to pull over to the parking area. We arrived and he told me not to shut off the engine. He hopped out and said, "You're ready for your solo flight. Take it around the pattern three times. After you land each time, taxi back and go around again." It's hard to describe the feeling you get when you are alone in an airplane for the first time, taxiing for takeoff. I remember pulling out onto the runway, pushing up the throttle lever to max and starting my takeoff roll. As I lifted off, I glanced at the empty right seat and let out an excited yell. It was at that exact moment I also realized it was all up to me. There was no one in the plane to help me if I got in trouble. It's amazing how our conscience level can rise to such a height in an instant. All my senses became in tune with that airplane. The human mind is more powerful than we can imagine.

Now when I sometimes fly the Piaggio Avanti II, one of the world's most aerodynamically advanced civil aircraft in the world, as a single pilot at 35,000 feet, I sit back and look around me. It's an amazing feeling to be 'floating' that high in the sky with no sense of movement and be traveling at over 450 miles per hour.

Even after all the studying and learning I've done in the aviation field, I still wonder if maybe there's a little magic helping us along. It's awe-inspiring to look out at this pencil-thin wing and think about what Bernoulli figured out so long ago.

Every man I meet wanted to be a pilot and most still want to learn to fly. They can share this dream with their sons or daughters.

My book on aviation is aimed at alleviating some of the fears of flying people have by educating them.

I get asked quite often by young people if they should pursue a career in aviation. My answer is always the same. Yes! But I also caution them to get a full education. Have a plan to fall back on.

What most people don't know is besides being a pilot and an author, I'm also an executive film producer. One of the titles I own is *The Pistol, The Birth of a Legend.*

It's the amazing true childhood story of basketball legend, Pete Maravich.

The movie is more than just a movie about basketball. It explores the father/ son relationship between Press and Pete Maravich. Press Maravich put a basketball in Pete's hands at three years old. It's estimated he spent 20,000 hours practicing. Think of Tiger Woods. His father put a golf club in his hands at three years of age and he became the world's greatest golfer.

Encourage your children at a young age to explore their dreams.

Focus on one thing and become a master at it.

"Desire, Dedication and Discipline."

Go ahead! Live your life in 3D!

(The movie can be found on my website www.thepistolthebirthofalegend. com or www.visserentertainment.com. The download version can be found at www.thepistolmovie.com.)

Safe travels,
Capt. David Visser

Writing/Flying Quotes

Continued from p.83

Hey, everybody—watch this!

— Every redneck cropduster's last words

If God had really intended men to fly, He'd make it easier to get to the airport.

— George Winters

In the space age, man will be able to go around the world in two hours—one hour for flying and one hour to get to the airport.

— Neil McElroy, 'Look,' 1958

While these above have been to show how far aviation has come and to add a little humor, we must always remember that:

"Aviation in itself is not inherently dangerous. But to an even greater degree than the sea, it is terribly unforgiving of any carelessness, incapacity or neglect."

— Captain A. G. Lamplugh, British Aviation Insurance Group, London. c. early 1930s

What's the hurry? Are you afraid I won't come back?

— Manfred von Richthofen, "The Red Baron," last recorded words, in reply to a request for an autograph as he was climbing into the cockpit of his plane

I have a feeling that there is just about one more good flight left in my system and I hope this trip is it. Anyway when I have finished this job, I mean to give up long-distance "stunt" flying.

— Amelia Earhart, departing from Los Angeles, California, for Florida on 21 May 1937. Start of her last flight

We are on the line of position 157-337 … We are running north and south.

— Amelia Earhart, last received radio transmission, while searching for Howland Island, morning of 2 July 1937

Do you hear the rain? Do you hear the rain?

— Jessica Dubroff, seven-year-old pilot speaking to her mother by telephone as the engines revved for takeoff, she (and her flight instructor) crashed minutes later in rough weather, 1996. The Federal Aviation Regulations were later changed to stop 'record' flights by small children

The cause in which they died will continue. Mankind is led into the darkness beyond our world by the inspiration of discovery and the longing to understand. Our journey into space will go on.

In the skies today we saw destruction and tragedy. Yet farther than we can see there is comfort and hope. In the words of the prophet Isaiah, "Lift your eyes and look to the heavens. Who created all these? He who brings out the starry hosts one by one and calls them each by name. Because of His great power and mighty strength, not one of them is missing."

The same Creator who names the stars also knows the names of the seven souls we mourn today. The crew of the shuttle Columbia did not return safely to Earth; yet we can pray that all are safely home.

— President George W. Bush, address to the nation from the Cabinet Room. 14:04 EST 01 February 2003

About the Author

Captain David Visser is a corporate pilot and has held the title of Chief Pilot for more than 10 years. He is also an accomplished aerobatic pilot, successful commodities trader and an executive movie producer and owner of several films. David was born in Worcester, Massachusetts and spent most of his childhood in Vermont. He holds degrees in Aviation Management/Flight Operations and Business Administration/Finance with independent study in the commodities market.

Contact David at dvisser@visserentertainment.com or through www.thepistolmovie.com.